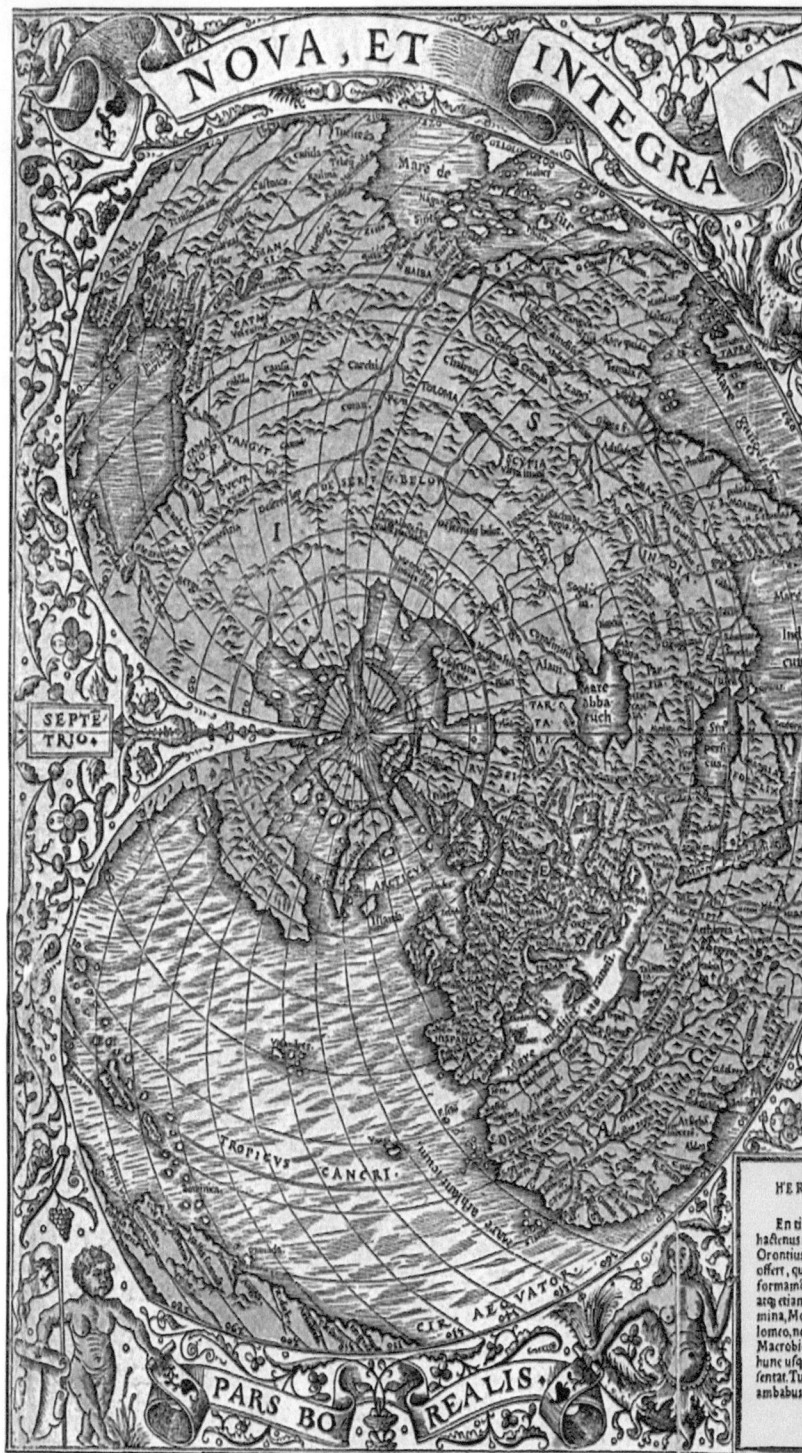

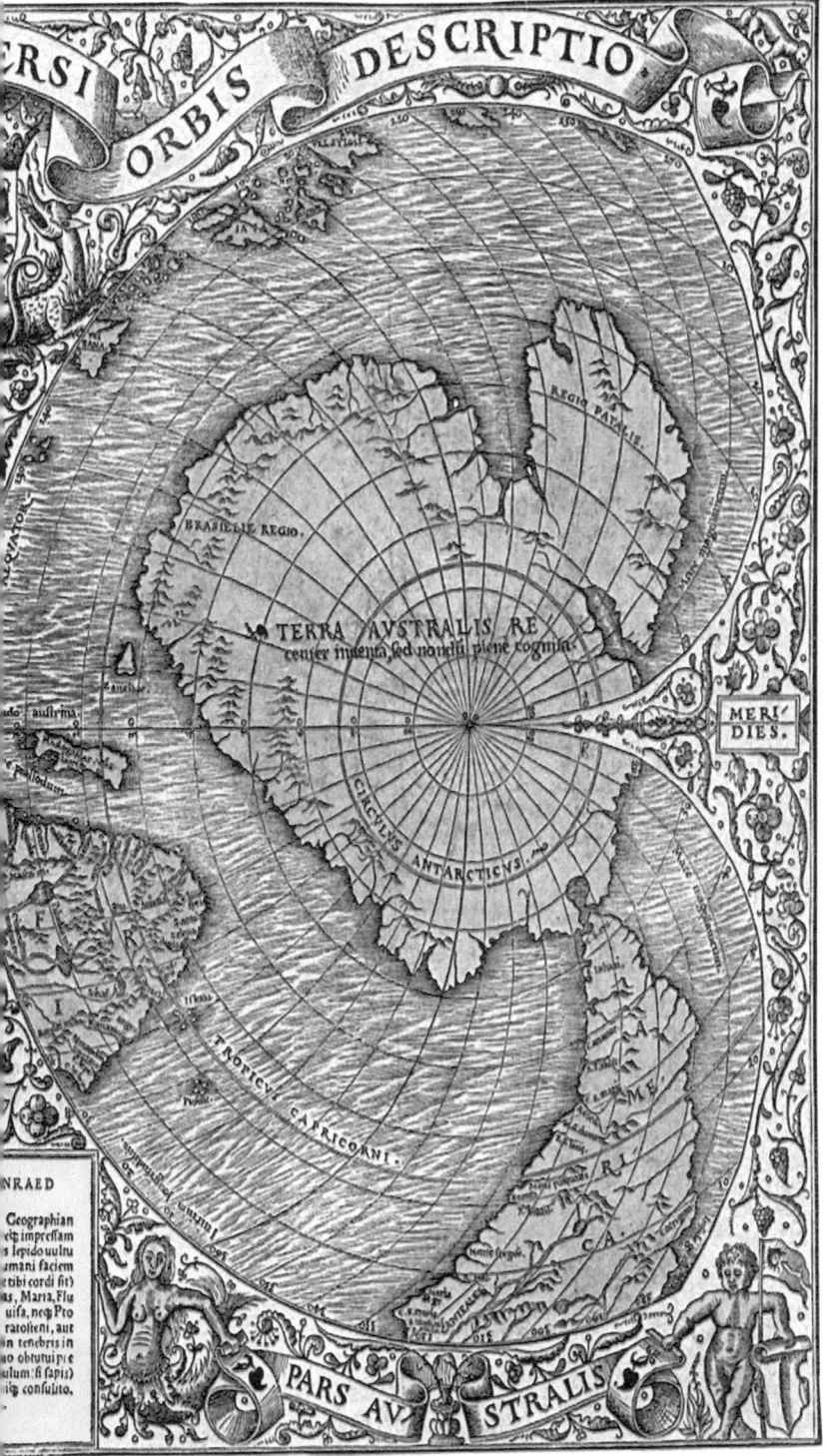

WALKING THE EARTH

Amina Saïd

WALKING
THE
EARTH

Translated by Peter Thompson

Preface by Hédi Abdel Jaouad

Contra Mundum Press   New York · London · Melbourne

Walking the Earth
© 2024 Peter Thompson;
Marcher sur la terre © 1994
Amina Saïd.

First Contra Mundum Press
edition 2024.

Library of Congress
Cataloguing-in-Publication
Data

Saïd, Amina, 1953–
Walking the Earth /
Amina Saïd

—1ˢᵗ Contra Mundum Press
Edition

144 pp., 5×8 in.

ISBN 9781940625683

  I. Saïd, Amina.
 II. Title & Note
III. Thompson, Peter.
IV. Translator.
 V. Jaouad, Hédi Abdel.
VI. Preface.

2024937639

TABLE OF CONTENTS

PREFACE

Errancy as Revolt & Freedom
On Amina Saïd's *Walking the Earth*

HÉDI ABDEL JAOUAD

Amina Saïd is the most potent — and prolific —
poetic voice in Tunisia today, if not in the whole of
Francophone Africa. She has so far authored some
twenty collections of poetry. Her poems have been
translated into several languages, and have received
overwhelming positive critical attention. Yet, for
some unfathomable reason no one has attempted
to translate a complete volume of her poetry, and
not for lack of choice or merit. Peter Thompson, a
poet in his own right, and an indefatigable and
talented translator of Francophone literature (es-
pecially Maghrebian) has with *Marcher sur la terre*
(*Walking the Earth*), her seventh volume, finally
remedied this jarring oversight.

Saïd's poetry is instantly recognizable: at once
simple, crystalline, and opaque, the quintessence
of the proverbial "complexity beneath a simple
surface." Typically, her poems are fashioned from a
few simple, everyday, elemental words and images,
constituting her basic creative materials, her es-
sential lexicon, and her singular poetic signature:
sky, earth, sun, star, exile, light, darkness, night, day,

desert, stone, absence, shadow, silence, sea — and an occasional horizon that lingers "patient" for the unhurried traveler, for "stilled walkers / keeping to the beat of their excesses." Such walkers are so rare that, oddly enough — in our modern world beset by frenetic speed & instant reactivity — they have become almost exotic.

With this elemental toolkit Saïd constructs a precise and concise language, distinctively visual and concrete, stripped of all rhetorical frills or ponderous thought, because the essential is in understatement, situated in the confines of silence.

From the unvarnished reality rises the poem: a poignant voice that often speaks aphoristically, resonant with strong yet subdued emotions, in a yin and yang dynamic movement of opposites and mutualization, which range from anguish and despair to ecstatic vision, suffusing the whole volume with a meditative, reflective halo, akin to the spirituality of mystical dervishes and Sufis, reminiscent of Rumi: "I am the place where I've fallen / I am the place I come from / and where I'm going."

Paradoxically, rendering Saïd's simple, everyday language in English is no easy task, beginning with the seemingly "pedestrian" title *Marcher sur la terre*, which literally means "Walking [on the surface of] the Earth." The overall meaning of the collection seems to hinge on these two words: "Marcher" and "terre," so pregnant with meaning and symbolism, requiring thus careful and vigilant contextual nuancing and difficult editorial choices, not to mention the deployment of the rich English lexicon of movement and mobility. "Marcher" and "terre" are thus consubstantial with each other, coextensive. Within the seemingly firm and stable sound of "terre" (earth/land/landscape/territory/turf/country, etc.), lurks, to the native ear, the resounding command "*erre!*," that primordial call for wandering and "errancy," which has been the human lot/condition since the beginning of times, and is a recurring leitmotiv in Saïd's writings.

The idiomatic expression *Walking the Earth* captures precisely and felicitously (more than the original title) the essence of this collection: Saïd's unwavering celebration of errancy as the highest expression of revolt and freedom. "Walking the Earth" is a journey, a way of life unburdened by material attachments, tantamount to a spiritual quest, often fraught with risk, hardship, and even terrible "ancient terrors [that] whistle through us."

The title invites us to reflect on the relation between walking the earth and the creative act. Inevitably, the act of walking leads us to the archetypal figure of *peripatētikós*, "he/she who likes to walk," and to think—to ancient philosophy and beyond—all the way back to the earliest records of thought.

More than any other of Saïd's collections of poems, *Walking the Earth* is steeped in archetypal, ancient images & founding myths. We embark on "a nomad night," on a journey that walks us back to the beginning, to the infancy of the earth, of the world, precisely at that liminal moment, between darkness and light, rupture and birth, to the moment that sets forth the creation of the sky & later the earth, & all life thereon: "all around / night and dream reigned / in primal form / from an uprooted sky / sun and moon were born / shadow light / and sap..."

It is quite revealing that in the beginning, there is no mention of earth, only of its mirror, an "uprooted sky." The first *earthling* to walk the earth, Adam, whose name means "son of the *red Earth*," appears belatedly in the poem, in the wake of the Flood; he appears under the guise of his most famous descendant, Noah, sometimes called the New Adam, the one chosen to perpetuate the human race after his contemporaries had perished in the Flood. In Saïd's version, Noah's story is intertextually conflated with the story of Jonah and the Whale, and that of the Arabian Sinbad the Sailor, "helplessly swallowed / by an enormous whale" and "in the doubtful cavern of its body / he found his sons their wives / and Sinbad the Sailor / hand frozen to his compass." The motley company, along with Noah's descendants, his "sons," escape the belly of the Whale, surviving the Deluge, only to realize that they are now mere mortals, suddenly confined in both time and space, finite "in the bowels of time/between birth and death," yet eternally stranded in a new and strange landscape, where they "saw nothing but land / and all there was to grasp."

Thenceforth, Adam-Noah's "sons" have become mere "errant stones," doomed, because of some Original Error, to eternal "errance," the very definition of the human condition: "wandering in the earth's wake / ill-suited to living / in the radiance of the world." Hence, the sense of inadequacy, "ill-suitedness" and restlessness, resulting from this ontological uprooting and displacement, that permeates the whole journey. Along the way, we meet a motley of lone travelers wandering aimlessly across "lost lands / found again / on the pathways of chance." These "travelers lost / in blank spaces" are also called passers-by, passengers, "one-way travelers," with "the impasse of faces," moving from "desert to desert," desperately in "need of a respite," of some desert oasis, with no end in sight, and no foreseeable future to contemplate: "our tomorrows / have the look of deserts / sown with emaciated wrecks."

By re-enacting our ancestral nomadic condition, Saïd simultaneously re-awakens in her increasingly sedentary contemporaries our common genetic impulse and sense of wanderlust, this urge to "regain the shore / of an unknown sea," to break from familiar habits & constraints, to experience the mysterious and the uncharted. But more importantly, she revisits, with fresh eyes, the familiar topoï of displacement and belonging, identity and alterity, and connections between the self and other people — especially between topography & (auto) biography — investing them with new meaning and contemporary relevance.

Even though Saïd's poetic world, essentially an ontological quest, seems to be devoid of local specificity, there are distinct flashes and echœs of "the childhood land," of an intimate filial experience sourced in the fertile grounds of her double heritage, a rhythm oscillating between cultures and languages across the Mediterranean, between the fatherland, Tunisia, and the motherland, France. In these echoes we hear the father's lament as he berates his child's exilic predicament, now a refugee on the other shore, "my father says / I'm in *the suburbs of death* / and the silence that follows / cannot still time."

More than any other poet of her generation Saïd's life writing is interlinked with place writing, and recalls Arthur Rimbaud, that cursed poet, the incarnation of the modern *peripatētikós*, the "Vagabond" "with the soles of wind," who, not unlike Saïd herself, had taken to "walking the earth" in a desperate and hurried quest to escape to an ever elusive elsewhere: "and we wandered, nourished on the wine of caves, and the biscuit of the road, I [who was] in a hurry to find the place and the formula" (Rimbaud, "Vagabond," *Illuminations*).

Ultimately, Saïd's poetics could be said to be a similar search for "le lieu et la formule," the place and the formula, and their interactions, for the "le mot juste / [that] strikes in the heart of hearts" and for the place one could call one's own, one that would put an end to the nagging question constantly asked of the wandering traveler: "what country are you from / someone asks / and where will your children be born." Ultimately, Saïd, like Rimbaud and other fellow "pèlerins de l'errance" [pilgrims of errancy] will make of wandering not only her place of election, but also her mode of expression, the language she will inhabit: "within its form / the poem seeks itself / love invents us / and speaks the senses' language."

Saïd writes about intimate, sensitive, and secret worlds dominated by absence and silence. But it is silence that best finds her voice, her register to express the depths of her emotions. Like no other,

Saïd gives voice to silence, parses the silence that lies at the heart of movement, so well observed by the ancient Chinese sages: "In all stillness there must be movement; in all movement there must be stillness" (a *Qigong* [ancient Chinese] saying). *Walking the Earth* is filled with both movement & stillness. The volume is framed like a mystery film, by a haunting, subterranean silence, and more specifically "white silence," its soundtrack: "death all around / is a white silence / commented by the gardens / a silence fathomless." This "white silence" drowns out all other sounds, inducing in the reader a sense of foreboding, of otherworldly strangeness, tension and confusion, yet all tempered by flashes of familiarity, serenity, and illumination.

Walking the Earth is a precious gem of book, full of metaphysical meditation and earthly wisdom, couched in a distinctively spare, sober but circular and captivating language that ensnares by its seductive clarity and simplicity. Saïd proves again that she stands apart as a poet with a cosmic ambition to embrace the World, to imagine it globally, a unique voice among her peers in the Maghreb and the Francophone world at large!

In Peter Thompson, Saïd has found more than a translator, but a kindred, soulful voice in the English language, a fellow poet who deftly captured every nuance, tone, and turn of her idiosyncratic writing, one uniquely endowed with a trained ear for rendering the cadence of the pregnant and fathomless silence that suffuses this volume.

A NOTE

BY AMINA SAÏD

In *Walking the Earth*, my seventh book, which opens and closes with the word "place," I seek out a "place" that goes from the personal to the collective, from the intimate to the universal; it is the author's space, but also that of numerous people or characters in the book who go through spaces as much geographic as mental — people who are displaced, uprooted, hounded by wars and disasters, migrants as well as travelers, wanderers, those who merely pass by...

The theme of wandering is very present in Maghrebi literature. It is at the same time choice and destiny, departures and returns, all of which create the desire for "place." Hence the image of the writer as forced like a tight-rope walker to advance above an abyss. The source, also, of the impression of betweenness — possibly a privileged situation for a writer.

So writing has made possible for me an intermediary position between two worlds — Occident and Orient, and the two shores of the Mediterranean that I belong to, a "place without place" where the feeling of difference while also belonging is reinforced, a space where identity is forged.

My belonging to these two worlds both legitimizes the quest for place and generates a proliferation of doubles: shadows, voices, witnesses, angels, those who keep vigil…

This quest for place is born of a profound feeling of exile. Isn't any creative person "exiled," a nomad, an eternal wanderer seeking a place — a utopia, a place imaginary, impossible, dreamed of — which poetry can, with a sudden flaring, show in an unforeseeable image? A symbolic place thanks to which any feeling of exile will be abolished, where a being might arrive at a kind of unity. An "elsewhere" that evokes in us a sense of the sacred, a desire to accede to transcendence, an elsewhere that responds to a deeply spiritual aspiration and merges with the search for self.

These poems remain haunted by birthplace, the "other shore" of the Mediterranean, the original place that links to childhood & irrigates memory. So writing becomes a return to that non-temporal episode which is childhood. Distance from those landscapes perhaps explains their obstinate resurgence through and in my writing, as if I am trying to remain inscribed in them, with memory serving to fill the hollows of absence. And absence, this other name for exile, when it is positive, can open onto a new birth — "*and out of my own absence / I am born to myself.*"

This place of origin also conserves memories of ancient civilizations born on the other shore — the legends and myths that several poems refer to — while I, the author, remain sensitive to the time-less, the immemorial, all the dimensions of time itself: the dove priestess in the days of Carthage, or the seven sleepers in the cave.

Thus, across distances (spatial, temporal), the springs well up again in us because they have been in us always. Memory, and writing, allow us to pre-serve the past in the present; the poem becomes a return, even when we are in constant renewal, a renewal which will push us ever forward, willing our motion — for which the book's title also serves as metaphor.

WALKING THE EARTH

To G.

all around
night and dream reigned
in primal form

from an uprooted sky
sun and moon were born
shadow light
and sap

and this desire to create
amid fire and tears

the uprooted sky
we were able you and I
to walk the earth

the mot juste
strikes in the heart of hearts

the horizon is patient
for stilled walkers
keeping to the beat of their excesses

we abandoned villages
to settle in the space
of a lone cry

a circle of bare stones
someone recites
our sad fables

we rekindle our embers
in black water
brandish our severed hands
at the sky

what country are you from
someone asks
and where will your children be born

where will you be
when under the clouds'
bloody smile
they fumble for a fleshy breast

all paths
lead to the same place
journey is illusion's horseback

the world's embers
blacken its wanton footstep

they burn
our anxious tongues

within its form
the poem seeks itself

it's this black water
that dazzles us

when we give it back
the far glimmer of a star

night settles over the day
we gaze full-eyed
upon life

love invents us
and speaks the senses' language

aureole of silence
before our lips

bringing us the echo
of a childhood land

the memory ceremony

we regain the shore
of an unknown sea

waves in succession
dissemble the heaving

and we will gather always
the night falling within us
like a black nail
into flesh's very flesh

ringed on every side
the day wears down unknown to us

it sculpts on our secret face
a singular mask

my shadow recognizes yours
your shadow recognizes mine

their rebel fingers
rifle the dark

looks exchanged
can only belong to night

guardian shadows
lying in wait for mirrors

like scolding birds
they unfurl rumpled wings

their formal shares barely touch
on their doubled nature

the precursor bird
symbol of what is to be
brings together water earth
and fire

an angel in the garden

my father says
I'm in the suburbs of death
and the silence that follows
cannot still time

in his image-language
the angel knows different

from the heart of the obscure
he follows the metamorphoses
of light

and his visible form
continues to express
the clouds

whoever has kept the night in suspense
for light or for a star

while we were stealing words
from joy and its opposite

in this way day is torn from night
and shadow from our eyes

they open yet again
renewing the pillaged
miracle

thursday or wednesday
at the twilight hour
a stranger
message in hand
will knock at the door

he will dally a moment
splattering ink
on the blotter's rose

the stains will form other stains
(cultivating a circle)
a face under the lamp
will rapidly blink

a woman's body will emerge
the one you love
always the same one always
different

there might be this body of light
for learning how to keep
death at a distance

out of the sun's path
and the untouchable fire
new signs would be born

a mirror remembering itself
would rediscover in me
what even I don't know

spread on the laughing rock
the days would blend together

and no face out there
for me to go seeking

once again
we're surrounded by fire

the uprooted star
turns its clairvoyant face to us

like a fire
nourished by another fire

this new moment
something pulses in us with life desire

something dies in us
and stretches in the depths of a tomb

this new moment the dawn
in all its truth
takes our breath away

the world around us
exhausts its definition

in the night the absent
and the separated join again
(so says the proverb
of free men)

they expect from the tree
chance survivor of the day
a measure of fruit
nourished by its light

they have the undamaged voice
and the incomplete face
of the living

out of one horizon another
absence of sky

disfigured circle
somber noon

a being
haunted by transparent birds

behind our dreams
our familiar shadows
(have they ever seen the day)

share of the invisible
is slice of moon

in the light stretched forth
the sun bears fruit in the glance

earth is this round dream

in its heart
stones fusing

their fire tongues
gouge the pathways of blood
where another fire burns

like a tree
balancing on the day
you dress yourself in birds

the light is weightless

in this body
what is it you seek

up against the wall
a mouth cries out

time is this face
refugee on the other shore

our place falls apart
like a lost mirror

a few carved stones
grooved by our tongues
augur not one
of the metaphors announced

among us
the disillusioned gods
have caught fire

radiant day
launches the mute cry
of its splendor

attentive to what is birthing
(breath clay flame)
over lifeless silence
we lay down a word

which calls forth another word

celebrating the transfigured territory
of absence

our anxious doubles
do not yet know
how to live in the world

blind to all light
our stone bodies
lying deep in the cavern

night place
where night makes a couple
with the night

room left for our shadows' rustling
our obscure doubles
wandering in the earth's wake
ill-suited to living
in the radiance of the world

site of the inspired tatters
of our history

site of rough beauty
of the branch and the fruit's bursting
and transient flesh

space left for the tower intact and
already higher than the flames
and of the fevered god who steps forth
he is soon finished off by the crowds
their panting humiliation
a knot slipping around his neck

site of the witness who arises
of the infinite burning
of his divined words

site of time awakening

lost lands
found again
on the pathways of chance

ruts sprinkled with stars

travelers lost
in blank spaces

on the page silence
conceives me

it is a winged secret
haloing the poem

our lips run onto reefs
of vowels

galleons of sand
siesta of suffering

the sky spirals
in its own fascination

birds feed
on the grain raised from our flesh

purple harvests
torn from ribs

we listen to the trees wailing

hands sated with steel
dead chain hands
of silences that hold forth

hands closed
on the stone's round cry
hands drained of the ink
of the self's blood

hands opening anxious space
hands amputated from childhood

in their cracks
the eye reading the implacable
outline of dying

knights gallop
through our heads

flocks armies
grave children
women rend their shirts

fishermen fling their nets
and contemplate the catch

a fruit splits open on the world

                        *

in our heads a scribe
enters the names
of past generations

before their slow migration
birds find rest

grains grown backwards
books lose their pages
doors open
doors close

trees grow tall
serpents coiling in them

men open fire
bodies scatter
walls crumble

terror crafts itself
a cozy nest

*

in our heads a cavern

an abundant woman
brings into the world and
then eats her children

without turning around
a man buries as many stones

rather sand than mud
say the stones
as they begin to talk

on a wall names dates initials
of the beings locked away here
count the days months
years

*

23

our heads
an ancestor awakens there
an ancestor falls asleep

gleaners bend
careful of their furrow
their sisters bake bread
for the voyage
and clutch stained eggs

others in silence wash
the night's dead

                         *

our heads
a camera films the insides

statues line up
fettered and blind

waves wear down their pedestals

above the void
a bridge is thrown

a voice sings
a voice calls out

a voice recites
a voice despairs
the choir takes heart

a hand inscribes
ancient alphabets

the light awakens

fire centered
between parentheses of shade

fire centered
like an assay of light

the hour is stretched
from window to window

it dries
in the day's fires

with wasted steps
time sleepwalks
advancing toward the end of time

this land that bears me along
a house with no master

one idol destroys the next
in this land that bears me along

in this land that bears me along
the soul recognizes the horizon

in this country that bears me up
the bodies born out of love
silt over

in its sky
the skiff of the moon
and its sacred face

a goblet of light
bulging eye of my night

do we know what the sands
restore of light

what earth restores of
sap

the cloud's restitution
of prayer

what a burning torment
fatally signals
in the wretched hollow of bodies

what shadow restores
of light's miracles
(as someone said)
it is everything that was ripening
on the sun's surface

and then the dawdling night
a discarded mirror
where bodies are confused

our masks take heart
at the day's muster

and spit their volleys of birds
feathers hollowed
like reeds of ash

we straggle through the foam
of impassable fords
our reserves of blood
stuck in the blue of our veins

our tomorrows
have the look of deserts
sown with emaciated wrecks

our shadows twist there
in a dry pain
we're doomed to suffer

a glow pulls us together
the better to see us wander

a desert gains
our lost orient

in silence we name
what the grimace of time deforms

the heart modifies its man
death at its task
separates him from a new season

we'll lose ourselves
we'll find each other

love is night's worksite
the witness returns to himself

tomorrow is that distress signal
where light learns all

and we will be
and be no longer

for Serge Pey

1

light dazzled
in the white immensity of silence

we see them coming
dressed only in their names

men women children
our speech

their empty husk
nailed to the skin of the trees

branches lap up
the iron-footed birds

the page gives birth
to its share of sky

the sea arises
in the mirror of the unforeseen

*

they see us coming
men women

in our arms children
strangling in ropes

our bones float cracked
on the foam of the stars

we're fleeing the fire the flames
ancient terrors whistle through us

our cries smooth out
the vast creases of the wind

the sands alert
our speech

all around us no one answers
doors close on us dire and again

*

hands in the stars
we walk beside the paths

the trees keep by us
in the stumps of the sun
a hatchet

blood and dust under our feet

we cover all routes
at once

a secret dog howls
in the bare book of the earth

she trembles and shifts
and drinks deeply of us

we survive
for other destinations

*

they see us coming
men women
our last children
distribute along the way
the ashes of their mothers

defectors and prey
of the world's asylum

the storm appoints us
to our speech

we breathe dead light

2

they make their way
men women children
by night and in the light

their lot of flame
is like an aleph of clarity

strange promises
the stars are witness
to unjust displacements

destiny bruises their veins
their mouths delivered not
from death

rebellious beneath their feet
the earth turns
as on the first day

3

men women children
stones in their hands

their hands bleeding
over an absence of land

fig trees bleeding
white tears

the impasse of faces
bleeding at the edge of wells

*

men women children
they come so far

the light hounded from their eyes
bleeding over the veiled arc
of a lamp

their lives punctuated by stones
bleeding over the burning thorns

*

men women children
a black choir
on the cliff of mornings

night bleeding
over the blue mirror of the day

the day's blaze
bleeding on the invisible

the hand blind to any trace
bleeding the bird
beneath the eyelids of the moon

*

men women children
hanged by the wayside

the mouths of their burned homes
bleeding over the ash of walls

the trees surrounding
the wheat its stems
bleeding in a billhook of light

the worn wombs of mothers
bleeding ancestral pain

bent on their orbits
the stars of their coming death
pushing back the sky

4

they walked so long
men women children
in the straits of time
no one can say
what road rolls infinite
for the travelers

straitened on the land
their hands spin threads of fear

approaching new country
silence shattered now they rave

men women children
hollowed by solitude
entire trees burn
in their flesh

strangers until death
their eyes kept wide

does their fate lie
in the glare
that suddenly makes day
blacker than night

on the world's tablecloth
a banquet of stone

the gates all fail to hide
that the gardens are bare

are they right or wrong
who come from the blue

toward the towns
that love not their night

driven from the world
the mêlée the riot

the bare chest
of the men marching
on the extreme slope of day

(where have the children gone off to?)

without a cry cities and villages
have disappeared swallowed whole
by the ground

(where have the children gone?)

a woman's shadow
contemplates the absence of colors

a flame licks at the eyes
the gaze must pass
through death's sieve

(where have the children gone?)

between the rings of sand
space is unbounded

out beyond there is nothing
but a smoke screen

no star can find shelter

the innocence of open palms
raises a flight of stones

see them live
in the blaze of the light

behind the window
a fire surprises itself dying

a man escapes
he approaches dream like a stranger

perhaps on the lips of stones
he'll find his image again

the riverbank bears witness
to places with no more days

like a first song
forgotten by the birds

the arc of blue mornings
plots against night

suddenly accomplice
in the neckline cut low by light
the land blazes up

in the empty house
a woman creates her child
set against death

bare palms and live matter
the wall gives when pushed
imprisoned bodies
turn to the day

like a blade
something slices the light

shrill flowers of blood
dance skyward from hands

drunk and distant
the bird of pure flame
darts forth in day's overture
and flies
far above time

severed hands
gather the grimaces
of dead fruit

severed hands unseal
the stones of houses

severed hands
stone the gaze of women

a madness encircles the walled-in
who set off on foot
in the nakedness of the paths

a last prayer before nightfall

a time will come
when the only witnesses
will be mute

blind to details
behind millenary masks

of what worlds
might they speak to us

night augurs long
and there we'll always be alone

or perhaps we'll never
be lonely there

artists of the impossible
we hardly belong to ourselves

our shadows weave illusion

with slow gestures
they feed on our dreams

they scream the space of an instant
rip the envelope of night

they rave and rifle through
their incandescent heart

what they need to find
is the petrified echo of silence

a despairing dawn
claws at the breast of night

beyond the gaping doors
furtive hands
have closed around
the massacred fruit of hope

hollowed by shadow
the rusted vessels
soon again take to the sea

the doormen of day
will have once again succeeded
in bolting shut the light

we didn't come
of our own accord
to the depths of the cavern

the earth gaping
above the abyss we fell
to its bottom

and look at us pale sleepers
lighted by an inexplicable fire

we are only a dream
in the darkness

as long as we haven't found
human voice again
our slumber stumbles on

sands
the first mirrors of night

the blond star is reflected there
bristling with arrows

suddenly a star
deploys its barbed wire

the angels light and cold
were three in number

weighted with stones
a body at the bottom of the water

breasts still young
and such long hands

two voices gave forth in her

why do you always
look me in the eyes
one of them asked someone
in particular

questioning her madness
the other voice said
there are two voices in me

there are two voices in me
who will tear her skin away from this world?

striding out
of the mud's embrace
is it the dead woman coming back

over her mouth
the seal of silence

just like the centuries
my old black goddess

a shadow surrounding her
heaves shovelfuls of fire
on the coal dust of gazes

we greet each other
with a doubled silence
before falling
under the blows of fate

tomorrow perhaps they'll bring us
back to our enigmatic shore

I will be that stone of light
my face furrowed
with tiny characters

the rebel song of women
throats of fire
timorous rumblings

the clouds fray
on nails in the walls

a country whose sands erase it

I leave one desert
for another

a rescued sun
hunting its synonyms
among sovereign mirages

what evil awaits us
the women ask

it's a doll's smooth stomach
escorted by the convoy

stomach like that lucky sun
seeking its synonyms

rain unhoped for
will sparkle in the wedding fires' light

*

wandering
over rocks in the sky

wrapping lightning
in the tree of sacrifice

the madwoman going naked
borrows blood's path

*

near the saint's tomb
my sons

death in the village
women and a body devastated

my sons
like errant stones

in a strange land
were my sons plundered

in the fire devouring its own wings
my sons gone up in smoke

my unborn sons
death covets them already

on the palm of my hand
my sons
insomnia in their gaze

my sons come to meet me
in my half-open gaze

*

let's go gather up the birds
(she said)

light
on foam's faltering step

in the still transparence
of the sun the pomegranate's
hard flower bursts

a stone body
quits the dreamy sarcophagus

the dove priestess
traces the sign of ash
of dust

her arms' welcome
precisely reflects the smile
of the horizon

where the blue mountain
drinks deeply from the sky

birds of no birth
are still fleeing the night

a lamp goes out

tortured parentheses of the sky
eternal tree inaccessible orchards

until the evening
light will embalm
the secret folds of our solitude

subtly the oracle
the unforeseeable

tomorrow will be possible
if the day in us
comes late

to Abdellatif Laâbi

one-way travelers
we need a respite

(where there's doubt
truth erupts)

one-way travelers
on the deepest paths
of word

only a second's inattention
for us on this tightrope

our wings talk of soaring
the take-off is a hope of light

our star drifts away
on the back of infinity

night chiseled in silence
starry face
in a moony quarter

its light awaiting
a distant sun

and then the slow dawn
sap running in the pen

the sky sketches a landscape
in colors of its own memory

pensive pebbles
picked up along the shore

a woman in tears
in time's sphere

we are so many grains
in the haystack of the world

prisoner of the circle
the pacer returns
to his point of departure

(that's how he advances
his shadow by his side)

to the messenger night
his tremorless speech
is of ancient goddesses

from one sky to another
he sees only them

at his side his shadow
run through by passers-by
who are guilty of caring
neither about the love that forms us

nor about the charred beast
looking on

prisoner of the circle
the pacer returns
to his point of departure

(that's how he advances
his shadow by his side)

children abandoned
in virgin spaces

they look light
in the face

under the sleek vault of the sky
earth is a table laid out
as for a banquet

but the night that day follows
that night follows
that day follows
limns a perfect circle

at a detour off the path
they find a body stretched out

a body separated from its soul
body in the image
of its first slumber

will it matter to them to know
who it was

night illuminates
night where I enter

a circle swooned
in the manifold fire of lamps

hours skim over the inaccessible
(the time allotted
will not renew indefinitely)

faces retrenched
in the division of planets

our planet retains
its power of attraction
over the lively swarm of flesh

the day slowly arriving
unveils our every impatience

night shows off
fetters the landscape
with its trail of grief

it delights
in its innumerable eyes

its predatory beak
pecks a giant egg

it goes to meet
a woman without hands
biding in the hollow of the labyrinth

the egg blazes
as fully as the silence

here (says the dead girl)
there's no room for the heart

mirror where there dwells
this bright country this mirror

sovereign light
ruminates beyond the sands

nomad night
will stun you without proof

thousands of birds
will suddenly leave your house

this flame the only survivor
this nightlight

the foreseen matters little
the unforeseeable shapes the poem

one shadow tears
at the wings of ashy birds
on its bones it sharpens
the grey violence of iron

wounded the other believes it sees
a devastated sun
and with eyes shut dreams
of strange births

you're not really dead
(says the murderous shadow)
but the day in order to appear
needs your blood

and with one breath
it snuffs the tiny flame

suffering mornings
embraced by solitude

suddenly she brightens
at a friend's letter

it talks of the fruit of the wave
and the bird that lingers
bequeathing a reticent name
to memory's round pot

nothing will replace the sun
its ripe wing bearing us up

nothing will replace
the act that brings the day
mysterious obedience
to a lasting order

shot through with clouds
or their gleaming
the house of the big sky

a ladybug caught
in the barbed wire of the wind

someone knocks at the door
a fish disappears
under the plank of the table

freed from an old dream
a sea treasure
dwells in white nets

someone knocks at the door
it opens upon laughter
the sea breathes swell to swell

a ladybug is caught
in the barbed wire of the wind

two little girls
launch a fable
a star shines
on the sea's brow

winter shows november the door
summer readies its affairs

it's night and day at the same time

a witch overturns the season
flesh of a tulip
where the wellsprings bend

to be a bird a moon ray
a spray of wings or of light

1

when the flood came
noah embarked alone
on a thread of light

(anything else is a lie)

with his cane he struck at his sons
who tried to follow

the water rose imperative
in its black whirlpools
the sons disappeared one by one

noah expertly steered
that phantom boat
the animals survived
perilous metamorphoses

then noah was helplessly swallowed
by an enormous whale
in the doubtful cavern of its body
he found his sons their wives
and sinbad the sailor
hand frozen to his compass

they were all choking
from the lack of air

all sensing exclusion
from the dream of the world

in so much night the days
were indiscernible

they made a blaze
of their illusions

2

having lost its landmarks
in the vast liquid expanse
the animal wandered from its path
and in the end was stranded

fleeing the mirrors
hidden deep within them
men and women cleared
a laborious path
in the bowels of time

between birth and death

land and sky rustling with birds
and stretching out of sight

they however saw nothing but land
and all there was to grasp

and everything precisely everything
began again

next time you will die
by fire
boomed a familiar voice

once again the angels
tried to intercede

under a rain of sand
we will conjugate signs
and wild talismans

a woman from another age
will lean at the edge of time

to offer the day our dreams
bring together words
and set it all on fire (she'll say)

with its black roots the olive tree
will crack the rock of silence

a bird will bend the bough
a fruit will bend the bough
a body will bend the bough

marrying the echo
of dead seasons
wind will take the boat
to other landmarks

the eternity of the waters trembling
under an unstable moon

the sky holds on only
by the grace of stars

dawn's instant
will be that lamp
in the hollow of a palm

and then the hour will change
only on the clockface of the sun

as the light gathers
the root of things

thus we are
those who are dreamed by the night

those who see in every birth
a test of the highest order

those for whom love
starlights a rediscovered dawn

those whose memory travels
childhood as if through its own universe

those who can read in stone
as in the obverse of a landscape

those who tumble in time
like a body in water

those whom shadow abandons
for a different light

that's us

watchers astray in the night
nourished with our reefs
from childhood to childhood

our flames lively
our places without duration

our furtive voice
lost recaptured
never consenting

watchers lacerated by inhuman night

our lucid distress
our discoveries
scared of themselves

watchers with backs to the sea
rejoining the cradle of the void

ugraspable fruit
of our impulses

a bird has ripened
in the tree of evening

cistern orchards of moon
the sky is mirror
in the water's mirror

presences lost while our shadows
shape the clay
of our mad legends

night is still enigma
and we amble
toward no paradise

tightrope walkers on the infinite thread
bemoaning the calm impotence
of our mother-of-pearl wings

the certainty of the abyss
sets our word free
flickering flame

death all around
is a white silence
commented by the gardens

to the mark time leaves
on things
to fire to sands

to that which has been given
that which has been refused

to men who struggle on
to death hanging a moment
over them

to their black and constant twins
to our bodies that can't fly
to the thirst weighing down the drowned

to the still pathways of blood

I will oppose the angel
the chimera and the bird

the space lending us its wings
the blank paper of days
the confidence of the landscape

that which must exist
that which will be given

*

to the threats and the hostages
of a bad cause

to the storm's red galloping
to the dying wave
to the closed-off hours of now

I will oppose fable
brown bread stone and reeds
wild fruits of the east

the wave that lifts
love's moment

                            *

to the night before us
almost everything

the child's breathing
the grey dog the tree the poem

the march toward the light

the absolute of the instant

the glare of presence
the winged space of the page

that mental place
the madman in the garden

the lamp and the watchman
the house where they stay

when the time comes to say
I will oppose signs
the clearest of signs
and the most obscure

childhood laughed at time
not knowing the venom in things

later to build anything
they had to drift away from it all

adjusting our life
to the poem's test

let's keep from elevating too much
the narrow rhymes of our houses

denying presence
would kill us a second time

in the face of shadow
a fire stokes the wind's desire

guttering flame
in the flesh of symbols

the poems scents itself
with deepest night

I inscribe myself with sand and dust
in the nostalgia of a world
from before this world

I'm absent
from the mirror of the tribe

stars bend
over the night

our silent doubles
lay the surveyor's rods
of improbable births

they mold the great mask
the impatient dawn will wear
at the hour of alarms

in a vast black book
they inscribe the fervent words
of the reeling night

my shadow weighs no more
than an incandescence

than a fingernail dug
into the solar sap

than the blade's ardor
on the scales of the day

than its flesh reflection
on the blinded brow of night

my shadow tears off
its successive masks
rips its face upward

when it loses itself in me
it has only the terrible weight
of a dead body

I hold still in limbo
questioning all of life

passerby
of this earth you can inhabit
only what gazes at sky

in the great body of the world
I open the living way
that leads to other worlds

I hold still in limbo

you who come from shadow
will be prey to the shadow

you who love light
your luminous double
will reach the sun

the circle of all things

spaces that lack the winds' raving

our shadows contemplate
their unfinished state

on a slab of black marble
they rest their bare hands

I live only through my care
for light (one of them says)

and as it's getting late
this night
let us not take on bodies
before dawn the devourer of stars

already the bird enflames
the pure wings of the sky

flint under eyelids
limits submerged
the eye's opacity

all the world's light
at its first motion

and this surfeit of light
obscures the sky

behind the heavy smoke
as many blurred ships
who have lost the shore

condemned to the sands
the chapped mouth
arrives at a cry

a single stone
might inflame the light

shameless game of shadows

everywhere the void
up to the blinding sun
black the dominant color

bearing secret things
our shadows approach the reflection
of their own reflection

wounded agitated
with funereal passions

at their temples they wipe
eternal blood

here begins the very hesitation
that obliges them to live

flower and light
have the same root for us

thus does night pry open
great flowers of light

thus does night light up
beneath the sparkling strophe of the stars

then does every form dissolve
in the light and in the night

on the shore light unfolds
it is at last its own temple

the day barely born
wears the day's mourning

our night goes on
under the mental veil

light only
in the universe of the new day

and from my own absence
I am born to myself

this distance
from stone to star

and over the black water
back turned to the prow

the ferryman

murderer of shadow
regardless of life

drives the boat
of our night

noon
the hour is immobile

will we have to dislodge the sun

sacrifice to the fires of the day
white victims

strip our sleeping forms
of their false faces

the hour is immobile

the light likens us
to all the world's things

we succumb
to unknown voices

could we be powerless to retrieve
the axis of our shadow

*

midnight
the hour is immobile

invisible to ourselves
shot through with darkness

we draw near a different space
a time always renewed

night welcomes us
with other voices other forms
a silence fathomless

the hour is immobile

the star itself devoured by its shadow
does not oppose the black banquet

to dislodge it
will we have to sacrifice somber victims

guests of the night and for it
our bodies are no obstacle

in the earth's great fire
this perishable clay molded in our hands
is hardening

for what pointless conquests
have we entered
the volcanic sex of the world
its brief violent outbreak
its convulsed miracle where
a rose's obscure lip trembles

to unmask the silence
growing from a breath
and brushing against us before folding
invisible and secret

this hope encourages us

the birds look at us
they fall silent when we pass

as word upon word
we advance ignorant of the end
from knowing it too well

word upon word
their worried chain
in the uncertain thread

I am the place where I've fallen
I am the place I come from
and where I'm going

ACKNOWLEDGMENTS

The translator is endlessly grateful to Amina Saïd for kind permission and for much support along the road. Gratitude is owed, and heartfully given, to Contra Mundum Press for its impact and pro‑methean daring. Thanks also to the editors of *The Nation* and *Metamorphoses* for printing some of these versions.

COLOPHON

WALKING THE EARTH
was handset in InDesign CC.

The text font is *BC Figural*.

The display font is *BC Figural*.

Book design *&* typesetting: Alessandro Segalini

Cover design: CMP

Image credit: Orontius Finæus, *Nova, et Integra
Universi Orbis Descriptio* (Paris, 1531). Woodcut,
290 × 420 mm.

Cover image credit: Abdellatif Laâbi,
Untitled (2023).

WALKING THE EARTH
is published by Contra Mundum Press.

Contra Mundum Press   New York · London · Melbourne

CONTRA MUNDUM PRESS

Dedicated to the value & the indispensable importance of the individual voice, to works that test the boundaries of thought & experience.

The primary aim of Contra Mundum is to publish translations of writers who in their use of form and style are *à rebours*, or who deviate significantly from more programmatic & spurious forms of experimentation. Such writing attests to the volatile nature of modernism. Our preference is for works that have not yet been translated into English, are out of print, or are poorly translated, for writers whose thinking & æsthetics are in opposition to timely or mainstream currents of thought, value systems, or moralities. We also reprint obscure and out-of-print works we consider significant but which have been forgotten, neglected, or overshadowed.

There are many works of fundamental significance to *Weltliteratur* (& *Weltkultur*) that still remain in relative oblivion, works that alter and disrupt standard circuits of thought — these warrant being encountered by the world at large. It is our aim to render them more visible.

For the complete list of forthcoming publications, please visit our website. To be added to our mailing list, send your name and email address to: info@contramundum.net

Contra Mundum Press
P.O. Box 1326
New York, NY 10276
USA

2012   *Gilgamesh*
Ghérasim Luca, *Self-Shadowing Prey*
Rainer J. Hanshe, *The Abdication*
Walter Jackson Bate, *Negative Capability*
Miklós Szentkuthy, *Marginalia on Casanova*
Fernando Pessoa, *Philosophical Essays*
2013   Elio Petri, *Writings on Cinema & Life*
Friedrich Nietzsche, *The Greek Music Drama*
Richard Foreman, *Plays with Films*
Louis-Auguste Blanqui, *Eternity by the Stars*
Miklós Szentkuthy, *Towards the One & Only Metaphor*
Josef Winkler, *When the Time Comes*
2014   William Wordsworth, *Fragments*
Josef Winkler, *Natura Morta*
Fernando Pessoa, *The Transformation Book*
Emilio Villa, *The Selected Poetry of Emilio Villa*
Robert Kelly, *A Voice Full of Cities*
Pier Paolo Pasolini, *The Divine Mimesis*
Miklós Szentkuthy, *Prae, Vol. 1*
2015   Federico Fellini, *Making a Film*
Robert Musil, *Thought Flights*
Sándor Tar, *Our Street*
Lorand Gaspar, *Earth Absolute*
Josef Winkler, *The Graveyard of Bitter Oranges*
Ferit Edgü, *Noone*
Jean-Jacques Rousseau, *Narcissus*
Ahmad Shamlu, *Born Upon the Dark Spear*
2016   Jean-Luc Godard, *Phrases*
Otto Dix, *Letters, Vol. 1*
Maura Del Serra, *Ladder of Oaths*
Pierre Senges, *The Major Refutation*
Charles Baudelaire, *My Heart Laid Bare & Other Texts*
2017   Joseph Kessel, *Army of Shadows*
Rainer J. Hanshe & Federico Gori, *Shattering the Muses*
Gérard Depardieu, *Innocent*
Claude Mouchard, *Entangled — Papers! — Notes*

SOME FORTHCOMING TITLES

AGRODOLCE SERIES ÆD

HY PERION

On the Future of Æsthetics   2006–PRESENT

To read samples and order current & back issues of *Hyperion*,
visit contramundumpress.com/hyperion
Edited by Rainer J. Hanshe & Erika Mihálycsa (2014 ~)

CONTRA MUNDUM PRESS

is published by Rainer J. Hanshe
Typography & Design: Alessandro Segalini
Publicity & Marketing: Alexandra Gold
Fundraising & Grant Writing: Madeline Hausmann
Ebook Design: Carlie R. Houser

THE FUTURE OF KULCHUR

THE PROJECT

From major museums like the MoMA to art house cinemas such as Film Forum, cultural organizations do not sustain themselves from sales alone, but from subscriptions, donations, benefactors, and grants.

Since benefactors of Peggy Guggenheim's stature are rare to come by, and receiving large grants from major funding bodies is an infrequent and unreliable source of capital, we seek to further our venture through a form of modest support that is within everyone's reach.

Although esteemed, Contra Mundum is an independent boutique press with modest profit margins. In not having university, state, or institutional backing, other forms of sustenance are required to move us into the future.

Additionally, in the past decade, the reduction of the purchasing budgets across the nation of both public and private libraries has had a severe impact upon publishers, leading to significant decreases in sales, thereby necessitating the creation of alternative means of subsistence.

Because many of our books are translations, our desire for proper remuneration is a persistent point of concern. Even when translators receive grants for book projects, the amount is often insufficient to compensate for their efforts, and royalties, which trickle in slowly over years, are not a reliable source of compensation.

WHAT WILL BE DONE

With your participation we seek to offer writers and translators greater compensation for their work, and in a more expeditious manner.

Additionally, funds will be used to pay for translation rights, basic operating expenses of the press, and to represent our writers and translators at book fairs.

If the means exist, we will also create a translation residency, providing opportunities to both junior and more established translators, thereby furthering our cultural efforts.

Through a greater collective and the cultural commons of the world, we can band together to create this constellation and together function as a patron for the writers and artists published by CMP. We hope you will join us in this partnership.

Your patronage is an expression of your confidence and belief in visionary literary work that would otherwise be exiled from the Anglophone world. With bookstores and presses around the world struggling to survive, and many even closing, joining the Future of Kulchur allows you to be a part of an active force that forms a continuous *&* stable foundation which safeguards the longevity of Contra Mundum Press.

Endowed by your support, we can expand our poetics of hospitality by continuing to publish works from many different languages and reflect, welcome, and embrace the riches of other cultures throughout the world. To become a member of any of our Future of Kulchur tiers is to express your support of such cultural work, and to aid us in continuing it. A unified assemblage of individuals can make a modern Mæcenas and deepen access to radical works.

The Oyster ($2/month)

- Three issues (PDFs) of your choice of our art journal, *Hyperion*.
- 15% discount on all purchases (for orders made directly through our site) during the subscription term (one year).
- Impact: $2 a month contributes to the cost to convert a title to an ebook and make it accessible to wider audiences.

Paris Spleen ($5/month)

- Receive $35 worth of books or your choice from our back catalog.
- Three issues (PDFs) of your choice of our art journal, *Hyperion*.
- 18% discount on all purchases (for orders made directly through our site) during the subscription term (one year).
- Impact: $5 a month contributes to the cost purchasing new fonts for expanding the range of our typesetting palette.

Gilgamesh ($10/month)

- Receive $70 worth books of your choice from our back catalog.
- 4 PDF issues of our magazine *Hyperion*.
- A quarterly newsletter with exclusive content such as interviews with authors or translators, excerpts from upcoming titles, publication news, and more.
- 20% discount on all merchandise (for orders made directly through our site) during the subscription term (one year).
- Select images of our books as they are being typeset.
- Impact: $10 a month contributes to the production and publication of *Hyperion*, encouraging critical engagement with art theory *&* æsthetics and ensuring we can pay our contributors.

The Greek Music Drama ($25/month)

- Receive $215 worth of books.
- 5 PDF issues of *Hyperion* ($25 value).
- A quarterly newsletter with exclusive content such as interviews with authors or translators, excerpts from upcoming titles, publication news, and more.
- 25% discount (for orders made directly through our site) on all merchandise during the subscription term (one year).
- Impact: $25 a month contributes to the cost of designing and formatting a book.

CITIZEN ABOVE SUSPICION ($50/month)

- Receive $525 worth of books.
- 6 PDF issues of *Hyperion* ($30 value).
- 1 tote.
- A quarterly newsletter with exclusive content such as interviews with authors or translators, excerpts from upcoming titles, publication news, and more.
- 30% discount on all merchandise (for orders made directly through our site) during the subscription term (one year).
- Select one forthcoming book from our catalog and receive it in advance of release to the general public.
- Impact: $50 a month contributes to editorial & proofreading fees.

CASANOVA ($100/month)

- Receive $1040 worth of books.
- 7 PDF issues of *Hyperion* ($30 value).
- 1 tote.
- A quarterly newsletter with exclusive content such as interviews with authors or translators, excerpts from upcoming titles, publication news, and more.
- 35% discount on all merchandise (for orders made directly through our site) during the subscription term (one year).
- A signed typeset spread from two forthcoming books.
- Select two forthcoming books from our catalog and receive them in advance of release to the general public.
- Impact: $100 a month contributes to the cost of translating a book, therefore supporting a translator in their craft & bringing a new work & perspective to Anglophone audiences.

Cybernetogamic Vampire ($200/month)

- Receive $2020 worth of books.
- 10 PDF issues of *Hyperion* ($50 value).
- 1 tote.
- A quarterly newsletter with exclusive content such as interviews with authors or translators, excerpts from upcoming titles, publication news, and more.
- 40% discount on all merchandise (for orders made directly through our site) during the subscription term (one year).
- A signed typeset spread from four of our forthcoming books.
- The listing of your name in the colophon to a forthcoming book of your choice.
- Select four forthcoming books from our catalog and receive them in advance of release to the general public.
- Impact: $200 a month contributes to general operating expenses of the press, paying for translation rights, and attending book fairs to represent our writers and translators and reach more readers around the world.

To join the Future of Kulchur, visit here:

contramundumpress.com/support-us